ULTIMATE SECRETS FOR A HAPPY MARRIAGE

Roy John

Printed in the United States of America
First Printing: 2019
Roy John

ISBN- 9781792679179

Introduction

I'm very happy and excited to dedicate this book, to all those seeking to create a loving, fulfilling and enduring Marriage! This book offers 'powerful' and 'profound' relationship secrets and ideas, you can use every day, to create a truly joyful and fulfilling marriage. There are 365 unique ideas presented in this book. Each idea has the unique potential to transform your thinking and alter the very way, you view and approach your relationship with your spouse. The ideas presented are truly universal and can help improve and enhance your marriage, to take it to the next level .

As you go through the pages of this book, please allow time for the true meaning and profoundness of each idea, to sink into your consciousness. Soaking yourself in the depth and essence of each idea presented, will not only help you embody their essence but will also help you express them every day, in your marriage, with power, conviction and emotion! I recommend you read one 'Power thought' each day in the morning, when you wake up or in the night, before you go to bed.

Spend five or ten minutes to contemplate the essence of each 'Power Thought' and visualize the results you desire to see in your marriage. See in your mind what you want and feel as though, what you want has already become a reality! You can do this as many times as you want in a day and even write down the desired results you wish to see in your Marriage!

It's my earnest desire that, you understand and imbibe the true essence of each idea presented in this book and take positive action to make the ideas a 'reality'!

I have no doubt; the ideas will create a transformational shift in your thinking and you'll combine the shift in thinking with positive action and emotion, to manifest the desired outcomes you wish to see in your Marriage!

Wishing you the best married life, filled with, utmost love, fun, excitement, joy, fulfillment and abundance!

With Love,

Roy John

1

The greatest gift you have as a human, is your ability to create using your 'free will'. It means, everything in Life and Marriage ultimately boils down to your 'Will' to create!

2

Create a beautiful dream for your life together with your spouse and live that dream with passion every single day!

3

Your soulmate provides an opportunity for the 'true' nature of your soul to flower and blossom!

4

When you enjoy giving without conditions, you enjoy the purest form of love in your Marriage!

5

Don't look for 'Love' in your Marriage. Be the 'Love' you are looking for and you'll be lovable and loved!

6

When you believe you lack something, you operate from a state of lack, which makes it virtually impossible for you to create the abundance you are looking for in Life and Marriage!

7

You cannot bring about lasting positive changes in Life and Marriage, by just working at the level of your behavior. You need to work at the level of your mind, to bring about lasting change!

8

Acceptance is your best choice in this universe because, the universe is the 'Mind of the Divine' and everything that happens in it, is in perfect order!

9

Remember, how you treat your spouse every single day, is essentially how you treat yourself every single day!

10

Your joy in your Marriage depends on how much you 'give'. Look for more ways to 'give'!

11

The quality of love you express every day in your Marriage, not only determines the quality of your marriage, it also determines the quality of your life!

12

Every person on this planet has a strong and unquestionable need to belong. A 'loving' and 'inclusive' relationship is the only way you can fulfill this need in your Marriage!

13

Escape from the mundane as often as you can- just the two of you. It's amazing, what a change in scenery can do to your mood and relationship!

14

Just like water quenches the thirst of your body, Love quenches the thirst of your soul. Genuine acts of sharing and receiving, keeps your soul nourished with Love!

15

Remember, the only thing that stands between you and a beautiful Life, is your own FEAR!

<u>16</u>

True freedom in Life and Marriage, does not lie in your ability to choose *'what you like'* but in your ability to choose *'what is right'*!

17

'Love' is your best choice in Life and Marriage. It heals both the giver and the receiver, while 'Hate' hurts them both!

18

When you know the depth of what Love offers you every single moment you live, you'll have no choice but to offer Love, every single moment!

19

It's never about being 'right' in a relationship. It's always about being 'kind'. When faced with a choice, always choose to be 'kind'!

<u>20</u>

Your Marriage is built on 'emotional' bonds and not 'logical' bonds. Focus on emotional bonding with your spouse, to build a strong relationship!

21

Pay attention to things that bother you in your relationship. They'll often lead you to things 'within' yourself that need healing!

22

The quality of choices
you make every day,
greatly influences the
quality of your marriage.
Pay attention to the
choices you make every
day, to enhance the
quality of your Marriage!

23

Keep the feelings of excitement and romance alive in your Marriage by continuing to 'discover' and 're-discover' the reasons you fell in love with each other and chose a life together!

<u>24</u>

You are 100% responsible for the 'health' of your Marriage. Love is the vital nutrient that keeps it healthy!

25

Give your spouse your best love today. There is no guarantee you'll get a chance to give your best love tomorrow!

26

The Love you
'withhold' is lost forever.
The Love you 'give' is
forever gained!

27

The most important relationship in this world is your relationship with yourself. Your Marriage is just an extension of this relationship!

28

The best way into your partner's heart is through things he or she loves and admires. Talking and doing things he or she loves and admires, is a sure-fire way into his or her heart!

29

Be an 'Encourager'
and not a 'Critic' in your
relationship.
Encouragement
strengthens your
relationship, while
Criticism weakens it!

30

The true measure of your love for your spouse is not 'words' but 'actions'!

31

Do your relationship a 'big' favor by responding with 'little' favors for your spouse, every time he or she makes a bid for connection and attention!

<u>32</u>

The 'need to be heard' is a universal need. When you simply learn to listen, you'll simply improve the quality of your Marriage!

33

Your Marriage is like grains of sand in your hand. Held loosely with love and freedom, it remains. Held tightly with control and restriction, it slips away!

34

Without the fragrance of appreciation, your Marriage becomes stale. Make it a point to appreciate or call out something you noticed in your spouse every single day!

35

Your role in your Marriage is not to get your spouse interested in you. Your role is to become interested in your spouse!

36

Perfection is an illusion of the ego. When you let go the illusion of perfection, you'll see your Marriage becoming more perfect!

37

You play your 'true' role in your Marriage when your spouse's happiness becomes as important to you, as your own!

38

You cannot have a good Marriage, if you are focused always on winning. Remember, where there is a winner, there is a loser. Always think Win-Win!

39

Don't reserve your celebrations for just Big things. Learn to celebrate small things and have fun together as a couple, to make your relationship more fun and enjoyable!

<u>40</u>

As the sun melts away ice, kindness melts away misgivings in your Marriage!

41

Remember, sorrows shared in your Marriage are halfed and Joys shared are doubled!

42

Be careful of the walls you build in your Marriage. They could soon become your lonely prison!

43

A mind possessed by the ego, is a mind that is imprisoned by itself. It creates pain and suffering, completely unaware of its own freedom and believes it is not free!

44

You spouse may forget what you said, but he or she will never forget how you made him or her feel!

45

Alone, you are One.

Together, you are a Team!

46

You get annoyed or offended by things your partner does or says, when some part of you feels threatened. Remember, anything that can be threatened is not 'real' and anything that is not real does not exist!

47

Like the morning light peels away the darkness of the night, a sunny smile is often all it takes to peel away the darkness of a strained Marriage!

48

When you find true joy and happiness in the expression of your partner's best qualities and talents, you make your Marriage a true abode of love and happiness!

49

Your Marriage is a new world waiting to explored and enjoyed. How much of it you explore and enjoy, is totally up to you!

50

A loving mind is aligned with the wisdom and possibilities of the universe and achieves 'everything' worthwhile. An unloving mind is aligned with the fears and limitations of the Ego and achieves 'nothing' worthwhile!

51

The abundance of love you share in any given moment in your relationship, depends on the abundance of love you experience within yourself in any given moment. Remember, the source of Love and Abundance exists within You!

52

The feeling of 'oneness' and 'togetherness' is what everyone craves in a relationship. Find ways to bolster feelings of 'oneness' and 'togetherness'!

53

Difficult times test the strength of your relationship. Without them, you'll never know, how strong your relationship is!

54

In a 'Loving' Marriage 'Love' is your only choice!

55

A quality Marriage require spending quality time together. Make sure to spend quality time with each other to show you 'care'!

56

People in the 'best' Marriage, are people who are 'best' friends. Moving from the '*Best Spouse*' mindset to the '*Best Friend*' mindset, will make a world of difference in your marriage!

57

Keep the excitement alive in your Marriage by keeping the 'surprises' alive!

58

Treat your Marriage

like the most beautiful

and amazing thing on

this planet, if you want it

to be, the most beautiful

and amazing thing on

this planet!

59

You express your purest love in a relationship, when you give without a speck of expectation of receiving anything in return!

60

When you allow the light of love from your inner most being, to illuminate your mind, you illuminate every thought and action with the power of the universe!

61

In Life and Marriage, you always have only two choices - One that results in peace and happiness and the other that results in pain and suffering – The choice is obvious for anyone with the right mind!

62

You enjoy life to the fullest, only when you know the difference between the 'Real' and 'Unreal'. Remember, all things 'Real' can only be increased by sharing!

63

Each second in a day, is a divine call to happiness. When you heed the call, your body, mind and spirit are healed and made whole!

64

The universe intended creation to be, the ultimate expression of its own true nature and essence. You become a co-creator with the universe, when you express your ultimate nature and essence through your creations!

65

Remember, the universe designed Joy, Love, Peace and Abundance in such a way that, you can only keep them in your life by sharing them!

66

Realize how good your Marriage is when things are together, before it is too late to realize, after things fall apart!

67

Remember, without a relationship, you'll have no one to share your love and no one to receive love from!

68

Love is the ultimate expression of your soul's highest nature. Your ultimate calling in this life, is the expression of your soul's highest nature!

69

Your spouse cannot read your mind or know your feelings. Make sure to let him or her know what you are thinking and how you are feeling!

70

The more passion and ideas you bring to your Marriage, the more richer and abundant your relationship becomes!

71

When you make your spouse feel 'wanted', you'll become the most 'wanted' person in the world!

72

If you wish to create a state of love, joy and Peace in your Marriage, remember, you need to create that state in your mind first!

73

When you choose
'love' over 'hate' during
difficult times in your
Marriage, you choose
'miracle' over 'misery'!

74

What matters most in your Marriage is 'affection' not 'perfection'!

75

If you know love only as an emotion, your experience of life will be limited to just the emotion. If you know love, as the very source of life, you'll experience life in all its richness and fullness!

76

The greatest joys of life are beautiful memories you create in your Marriage!

77

Be the person in your Marriage who will be 'remembered' forever and not the person who will be forever 'forgotten'!

78

Your relationship with your spouse is nothing but a reflection of your own inner world. If you don't like what you see, fix your inner world instead of trying to fixing the reflection!

79

Instead of looking for a 'good' partner, be the 'good' partner you are looking for!

<u>80</u>

Few moments spent together in love is better than several moments spent apart!

81

Complete acceptance,
is what makes your
Marriage 'Complete'!

82

Explore the 'unknown' and 'what your Marriage could be', instead of being stuck with the 'known' and 'what has always been'!

83

A great Marriage is great, not because it has no 'problems', it is great, because it has 'solutions'!

84

Engage in open and loving conversations with your spouse, to keep the joy and fun flowing in your Marriage!

85

Continue to do what you did, when you first fell in love with your spouse to see your relationship continue forever and never end!

86

When you become willing to give what you seek, you become deserving of that which you seek!

87

Remember, vulnerability is an important part of a loving relationship. Without it your Marriage could very easily loses its charm and excitement!

88

Make every moment you spend with your spouse the best moment of his or her life and he or she will be yours forever!

89

A true and loving Marriage has a beginning but no ending!

<u>90</u>

When you love your spouse for who he or she is, you will be loved for who you are!

91

Just like flowers need light to blossom, your Marriage needs the light of love. Shine love in your marriage every day and see it blossom beyond your wildest dreams!

92

Learn to value your 'spouse' more than the 'things' in your Marriage. 'Things' will soon become meaningless without a good relationship!

93

Your heart sees more than what your eyes see. The deeper you let your heart see, the deeper your relationship becomes!

94

Marriage is like a game of cards. You need the whole set of cards, with all the different shapes, colors and symbols to enjoy to the fullest!

95

Your relationship is not like an occasional breeze that comes and goes, it's like the air that maybe silent but always there!

96

In a happy Marriage,
you don't try to be
happiness. Happiness
just happens!

97

You start your
Marriage by 'falling in love'. You keep it going by 'staying in love'!

98

Be in your Marriage, not because you 'need' your spouse. Be in it, because you 'love' your spouse!

99

Need makes your relationship 'selfish'. Love makes it 'selfless'!

100

Keep the peace in your Marriage at all cost. It's the life blood of any relationship!

101

Remember, how you make your spouse 'feel', matters more than what you 'say' or 'do' in your Marriage!

102

If there is any room for pride in your Marriage, it's pride for your spouse and not for yourself!

103

Remember, it's easy
for you to 'get'
something you easily
'give' in a relationship!

104

Genuine 'care' is the heart of a loving relationship. Without 'care', there cannot be a genuine relationship!

105

Love 'shared' multiplies Joy. Love 'withheld' multiplies suffering!

<u>106</u>

Your relationship will flourish like you never imagined, when you accept your spouse's past, care about his or her present and support his or her future!

<u>107</u>

When your spouse tells you, you hurt him or her, it's not the time for you to defend your actions. It's time for you to do what is necessary to make the feelings right!

108

Your relationship is like a garden. The more you water and take care of it, the more beautiful it becomes!

109

A 'loving heart' and a 'helping hand' is the hallmark of a great relationship!

110

Fear is the result of a sense of separation you experience in your mind. When the sense of separation is replaced by a sense of oneness, the darkness of fear leaves your mind and you experience the divine light of love in your relationship!

<u>111</u>

The more truly you love your spouse, the more truly you'll taste Love!

112

When you love your spouse truly, every hour, minute and second of your life becomes truly timeless and eternal!

113

You cannot experience anything in life without 'Involvement'. The more deeply 'Involved' you are in your relationship, the deeper and enriching your relationship becomes!

114

When you fall in love with your spouse, you don't discover your spouse - You discover yourself!

115

Small acts of love you show in your Marriage, shows your spouse, small parts of him or her, he or she never knew existed!

116

You open up new and exciting possibilities in your Marriage, when you learn to say 'Yes' more often!

117

The most important person in your life right now, is the person you are with right now!

118

Use technology to build connection while you are away. Use it to build excitement and anticipation about things you plan to do together with your spouse, when you return!

119

If you love your

spouse…

Say it!

Show it!

Be it!

120

The best way to love your spouse, is not by changing him or her, but by helping him or her become the best version of himself or herself!

<u>121</u>

Life is a vast ocean of

love and Marriage is

meant to be a beautiful

expression of this vast

ocean!

122

Remember, a great Marriage is built on the strong foundation of a great friendship!

123

You are never too

young or old, to dream new dreams and try new things in your Marriage!

124

When you give willingly with your heart expecting nothing in return, you enjoy the purest form of love in your relationship!

125

Remember, not every problem your spouse brings to you, requires your advice or solution. All that you need to do sometimes is, to just listen and let your spouse know, you understand!

126

Choose a gentler approach to discussing problems in your marriage, instead of blame, attack or criticism. The way you discuss problems, not only determines how your conversations will go, it will also determine how your relationship will go!

127

A good Marriage does not just happen - You just make it happen!

<u>128</u>

The best apology in your Marriage is not what you say - it's what you do after you apologize!

129

Disconnect from technology and connect with your spouse personally, by spending devoted and dedicated time together every day!

130

Remember, no argument is worth winning, if it will end up costing you, your Marriage!

131

You don't need a reason to love. If you need a reason, it's not Love!

132

Focus on things you can change in your Marriage, instead of focusing on things you cannot change!

133

Remember, what you don't do matters as much as what you do in your Marriage!

134

Learn to uncover the 'soft' emotions, that lie hidden beneath your partner's 'strong' emotions like anger, frustration, etc. Uncovering your partner's 'soft' emotions, helps you understand and connect with your partner better!

135

When you try to control your spouse, you essentially throw your Marriage out of control, because Marriage is a covenant of Love and not control!

136

Talking about and appreciating your spouse's strengths, is vital for the strength of your Relationship!

137

Remember, there are no idle thoughts. If you are 'thinking' right now, you are 'creating' right now – Good or Bad!

138

Never complain about yesterday in your relationship. It can neither make your today nor your tomorrow better!

139

Remember, when you are afraid, you are deceived by your ego into thinking: what you are afraid, is bigger than you!

140

Your Marriage is a union of two beautiful souls, who came together, to create one beautiful world!

141

Focus on 'what you want' in your Marriage, instead of 'what you don't want'. You'll get what you focus on, regardless of whether you want it or not!

142

When you hold the light of love for your spouse in your heart, there will be no room for the darkness of fear and suffering in your relationship!

143

A perfect Marriage is where two people come together to love each other, knowing they are not perfect and work together, to create a imperfectly perfect world they both love!

144

The only way you can get answers to some of the puzzles of Life, is by asking questions. When you ask the right questions, you'll get the right answers!

145

Success in your Marriage is not measured by how much your life is enhanced by the Marriage. It's measured by how much the Marriage is enhanced by you!

146

Ignoring each other's emotional needs can drain your relationship emotionally. Make sure to attend to the emotional needs in your Marriage by making each other feel heard and loved!

<u>147</u>

Frank and open communication is a great way to strengthen the connection in your Marriage. Compliment and vocalize your feelings for each other and also be willing to talk about things that may seem bad or uncomfortable!

148

Your Marriage needs respect just like plants need water. When you keep your Marriage watered with respect, you'll see it grow and flourish, like you never imagined!

149

The quality of connection in your Marriage, does not depend on the quantity of time but on the quality of time spent!

150

No matter where you are or who you are in this world, remember, you can never lose your ability to love, because, 'LOVE' is who you are!

151

Tell each other what makes you feel loved and special, instead of silently expecting to feel loved and special in your relationship. Clarifying expectations makes attending to each other's needs fun and easy in your relationship!

152

You can seek Love all your life, but can never know Love all your life, until you truly LOVE!

153

When you Love truly, you release yourself from an 'unreal' sense of separation, fear and scarcity, into a 'real' sense of oneness, joy and abundance!

154

All miracles in life, are nothing but expressions of Love. A relationship filled with expressions of Love, becomes a haven of Miracles!

155

When you genuinely understand each other, your relationship becomes a genuine abode of love and understanding!

156

The foundation of a strong Marriage is the feeling you instill in your partner that, you'll always be there for him or her - No matter what, when and where!

157

Marriage provides you an opportunity to love the person, the universe figured you owe the most love to!

158

Learn to share the trivialities of life in your relationship to refuel feelings of warmth and connection in your Marriage. Remember, the very act of sharing, is more important than the specifics of what you actually share!

159

When you learn to love truly, you teach your whole family to love truly!

160

You can truly enjoy

your relationship, only

when you truly enjoy

bringing out the best in

your partner!

161

Listening to your partner's needs and concerns without judgment, is often, all it takes to solve problems in your relationship!

162

The least you can do in your Marriage is - to simply be there for your spouse when he or she needs you!

163

The depth of your relationship is not measured by its length. It's measured by the breadth of your love for each other!

164

The best way to know love, is to love someone. Remember, there is no greater opportunity to know love than your own Marriage!

165

Without a relationship, you could be a lonely person on this planet!

<u>166</u>

You are the artist in your relationship. Each day, presents new opportunities for you, to create beautiful master pieces!

167

Have no other

purpose in your Marriage other than, to enhance and enrich it!

168

Your Marriage will not last the test of time, if it's not built on the foundation of genuine love!

169

A loving Marriage

never loses value, beauty

or goes out of style!

<u>170</u>

You give meaning to everything in your Marriage, just as with everything in life. Remember, it's not your partner's fault, if you choose to give something the wrong meaning!

171

When you forget everything you give and remember everything you receive in a relationship, gratefulness becomes your only choice!

172

Nothing happens in your Marriage by accident. Everything happens by choice. When you make the right choices, there will be no accidents!

173

The best treatment you can give your Marriage is, to treat your spouse the best way you'd like to be treated!

174

An open and loving relationship can happen only with an open and loving heart!

175

True measure of success in your Marriage is not always the number of things you have to discuss every day but the number of things you no longer have to discuss every day!

176

When you truly cherish each other's hopes and dreams, your relationship becomes something to be truly cherished!

177

Instead of looking for a loving relationship your whole life. Dedicate your whole life to a loving relationship!

<u>178</u>

Arguments reveal 'truths' in your relationship, which could be used as stepping stones, to take your Marriage to the next level!

179

When you make yourself available for your spouse in times of need, you make yourself worthy of a good spouse!

<u>180</u>

When you keep the 'honesty' in your relationship, you'll keep your relationship honestly successful!

181

An extra ordinary relationship is one in which, two people come together to make ordinary things extra ordinary!

182

A true Marriage is your commitment to desire the highest good for your spouse as long as you live!

183

The best gift you can give your spouse is the gift of your undivided attention!

184

Spending time 'alone' to relax and be yourself, is as important as spending time 'together' in your relationship. Relaxation creates the mental space you need, to make giving and receiving Love and Care easy in your relationship!

<u>185</u>

A good Marriage is a commitment to always be there for your spouse, even though, you may not always be there with him or her!

186

In a loving Marriage, it's not about what's convenient for you. It's about what's convenient for your spouse!

<u>187</u>

You can either make yourself 'happy' or 'unhappy' in your Marriage. Making yourself 'happy' is far easier than making yourself unhappy'!

188

The best way to build closeness in your relationship is, to provide a safe place for each other to share your feelings!

189

A good Marriage is not about having the best relationship every single day. It's about building a better relationship with every passing day!

190

'Nothing' in this world is worth more than the 'peace' in your Marriage. Let 'no-thing' take away your peace!

191

A strong Marriage does not require two people to be strong all the time. It only requires one person to be strong when the other is weak!

192

A great Marriage does not happen between two people who think they are two. It happens between two people who think they are one!

193

The best way to understand your spouse, is not with your 'head' but with your 'heart'!

194

When you feel love for your spouse, you don't feel your spouse, you actually feel your own true self as your spouse!

195

It's amazing how loving your spouse, can put you in touch with your own true essence!

196

Remember, it's not your partner's job to make you happy. The only person who can truly make you happy is - YOU!

197

You can see, hear, smell, taste and touch beautiful things in your relationship but the only way you can feel their beauty is - with your heart!

198

You were born to love and to be loved. You are in a relationship, so you can love and be loved!

199

You will simply be happy in your Marriage, when you simply make your spouse happy!

200

The simplest way to multiply your happiness in your relationship is, by simply sharing it!

201

Every moment in your relationship, is a doorway to make your unfulfilled 'dreams' a 'reality'!

202

It's not about 'who' is right in any given moment in your relationship. It's about 'what' is right in any given moment!

203

Remember, a Healthy Marriage keeps your mind and body in better health than any exercise at a Health Club!

<u>204</u>

Don't let the grind of everyday life get the better of your relationship. Let your relationship get the better of your everyday grind!

<u>205</u>

Don't expect your relationship with your spouse to be like any other. Expect it to be uniquely different and enjoy the uniqueness, because, you are two unique people!

206

Remember, 'Small' acts of kindness you do every day, can make a 'Big' difference in your relationship!

207

An apology does not necessarily mean you did something wrong. It means, you are doing what is necessary to make something right!

208

One moment of selfless love can change one moment of your life. A lifetime of selfless love can change your entire life!

209

When you become more aware of your feelings and the feelings of your spouse, it gives you a great opportunity to consciously manage your own emotions and the overall flow of E-Motion (Energy in Motion) in your relationship!

<u>210</u>

How you feel within yourself at any point in time, profoundly impacts the state of your relationship. Learn to bring yourself back quickly into a state of feeling good, whenever you find yourself drifting away into a state of feeling bad!

211

A great Marriage is not about falling in love with your spouse once. It's about falling in love with him or her every single day!

212

That which changes is not real and that which is real never changes. The only way to keep your Marriage 'real' is with steadfast and unwavering love!

213

You can most definitely make your reality better than your dreams if... You have the courage, to take your dreams and turn them into something better!

214

If heaven is a place of unconditional love, your Marriage could become a 'heavenly' place with unconditional love!

215

If you expect your Marriage to be good every single day, consider how much good you are contributing to your marriage every single day!

216

When someone loves you deeply, they reveal their highest self to you. When you love someone deeply, you reveal your highest self to them. Your Marriage is the only place on this planet that gives you the opportunity, to reveal your highest self every single day!

217

You will live fully only

when you love fully!

218

When you set your Spouse free to be himself or herself, you set yourself free to be yourself!

219

You should love your spouse not because of who he or she is. You should love him or her because of who you are!

<u>220</u>

If people could die for a loved one in a relationship, you could most certainly live for your loved one in your Marriage!

221

Conversations are an important part of your relationship. Find time for face to face personal conversations every day, instead of always going places or doing things that involve little or no talking or listening!

<u>222</u>

Put all your body,
mind and soul into your
relationship, because the
universe put all of itself,
to bring you both
together!

223

You play your true role in your Marriage, when you awaken your partner's soul and make him or her want to reach out for more!

224

There can only be two basic motivations in your relationship: Fear and Love. Fear closes your heart to everything the relationship has to offer, and love opens it, to all the joy, excitement and possibilities of a loving relationship!

225

Without true love a Marriage has no true meaning!

226

When you understand the power of love in your relationship, the love of power loses its power in your Marriage!

<u>227</u>

Romance and Physical intimacy in your relationship, are not meant to be rushed. When you learn to slow things down, you'll not only begin to enjoy them more but will also find yourself wanting more!

228

Your Marriage becomes truly interesting only when you become truly interested in your spouse!

229

When you share enjoyable experiences together in your relationship, you enhance the connection and make your Marriage more enjoyable!

230

Always choose 'Love' over 'Hate' in Life and Marriage. Hate may seem invincible in the beginning, but it always fails in the end!

231

Just like, you cannot hit something hard without hurting yourself, you cannot stifle your spouse's freedom, without stifling your own!

232

Discuss and mentally re-live the happy moments in your relationship, whenever you feel like your relationship needs a fresh burst of positive refreshing energy!

233

Your partner's way of expressing love, may be completely different than your own. Spend time to understand your partner's love language, so you can appreciate the different ways your partner loves you and expresses his or her love for you!

234

Remember, small expressions of gratitude every day, will yield big dividends in your Marriage!

235

Your Marriage is a journey and not a destination. Let go your expectation to arrive and enjoy the Journey!

236

You often think, you are only responsible for '*what you do*' and not '*what you think*'. Remember, if your thoughts are responsible for what you do, your ultimate responsibility lies at the level of your thinking and not your action!

237

Remember, what you do for each other every day as expressions of love in your relationship, is more important than the feelings you have for each other in your Marriage!

238

If your mind is the source of all your creations, it quite naturally is also the source of all your mis-creations. Learn to examine your mind often to uncover thought patterns that have the potential to Mis-create in your relationship!

239

When you do new and exciting things together in your Marriage, you keep your relationship renewed and exciting!

<u>240</u>

Creating a fulfilling Marriage, is part of your own responsibility to create a fulfilling life for yourself!

<u>241</u>

Having mutual goals or projects that you and your spouse can work together, gives your relationship the much-needed sense of pride, achievement and team spirit!

<u>242</u>

You are a team of two unique individuals bringing different perspectives and strengths into your relationship. Remember, the value you both bring into your Marriage are truly - Your Differences!

243

When your spouse does something, you don't like or understand, talk about it and explore why he or she is doing what they are doing, without making any assumptions!

244

Remember, your ability to handle and manage differences in your relationship, makes all the difference in your Marriage!

245

Don't let problems and bitterness simmer in your relationship. Resolve them when they happen and don't allow them to boil over!

<u>246</u>

Be careful of what you sow in your Marriage. Sooner or later, you will reap what you sow!

247

In the absence of 'closeness' in a relationship, people often fall out of love. Make sure you maintain the 'closeness' in your relationship with regular attention!

<u>248</u>

Never undermine a good Marriage by underestimating the power of good grooming!

<u>249</u>

Remember, your willingness to apologize and make up after an argument, is very vital for the happiness of your Marriage!

250

Spending time 'apart' doing your own things independently is equally as important as spending time 'together' in your relationship!

251

It's easier to have a good relationship with your spouse, when you have a good relationship with yourself. Always, nurture and maintain a sense of good self-respect and self-esteem!

252

Marriage exists for Love and Love exists for Marriage!

253

Marriage is a two-way street– with much give and take. That's the only way it's designed to work and it cannot work any other way!

254

Always stay open to spontaneity in your relationship and allow room for surprises!

255

Good physical, mental and emotional health is vital for a healthy Marriage. Do everything you can, to stay physically, mentally and emotionally healthy!

256

All relationships have their ups and downs and don't always ride at a continuous high. Learn to ride the high and low tides together as a team, to make your Marriage stronger!

257

Use your relationship as a mirror to see things within yourself, that need fixing!

258

Your Marriage is complete, only when you and your spouse enjoy complete 'freedom' in your relationship!

259

Laugh together often to keep your relationship lively and vibrant. The playful energy of laughter help alleviates stress and fosters a greater sense of togetherness in your Marriage!

260

A real Marriage is never perfect and a perfect Marriage is never real!

261

Love is not an absolute or finite commodity you give and take in your relationship. It's the endless ocean of Life and the purest essence of all Existence. How much of it finds expression in your marriage, depends entirely on how much of it you are willing to express through YOU!

262

Never ignore the power of Physical intimacy, regardless of the age of your Marriage. It's healthy and provides all kinds of biological and emotional benefits, that leads to a better and more fulfilled relationship!

263

Your Marriage needs more 'Excitement' than 'pleasantness' for improved marital satisfaction. Keep the 'Excitement' going in your relationship by regularly trying new things and sharing new experiences together with your spouse!

<u>264</u>

You choose 'monotony' over 'variety' when you try to change your spouse to become like you. What you need in your Marriage is 'variety' not 'monotony'!

<u>265</u>

Never threaten to leave your marriage. It weakens your resolve to stay and will have a negative impact on your relationship. Marriage is a lifelong relationship - Make sure to stay true to your commitment!

266

True Love offers freedom from the pain and suffering of your Ego. A loving relationship is your doorway to that freedom!

267

You don't need *'anything'* outside yourself to be happy because *'everything'* you need to be happy is inside you!

268

Practice non-judgment in your marriage. Judgment diminishes your capacity to love and reduces your ability to live life to your fullest potential!

269

You often say 'Thank You' for the 'big things' your partner does but forget to show gratitude for the 'little things' he or she does every day, to keep things together and flowing. Remember, gratitude is the single biggest contributor of quality in your relationship!

270

Every fire in your relationship needs to be stroked, to keep the excitement alive in your Marriage. Find ways to pepper your everyday routines with moments of novelty, fun and unpredictability to keep the excitement alive!

271

You cannot get good at something you don't continually practice. Find new ways to continually practice expressions of love, so you can get really good at loving!

272

What makes life worth living, is Love. What makes Marriage worth living for, is also Love!

273

Remember, the only thing you'll take with you when you die, is the love you gave away when you were alive!

274

Just like the limitless sky above you, the Love within you has no limits!

275

Love is the greatest miracle of Life that can make your Marriage miraculous!

276

With 'love', everything is possible. When you truly love, you make the impossible truly possible!

277

Love heals the 'receiver' and the 'giver' and everything it touches in your Marriage!

278

The best way to set the stage every day for a fulfilling relationship is, to wake up every day with a heart full of thanks, for a new day to love with a full heart!

279

'Patience' is the ultimate vehicle of Love that can take your Marriage places!

280

'Trust' is the highest tribute you can give your spouse. Without trust, nothing meaningful can happen in your Marriage!

281

Love does not happen in your Marriage by Chance. It happens by Choice!

282

The true meaning of life reveals itself to you, only when you truly love!

283

The only way to explore and know the depths of Love is by going deeper!

284

Without Love

'Everything' you have in your life amounts to 'Nothing'!

285

Without the true expression of love, the true beauty of your soul remains hidden!

<u>286</u>

Every expression of Love in your relationship, rekindles the divine light that lights up your Marriage!

287

You'll enjoy a mutually beneficial and fulfilling relationship with your spouse, when you seek to serve rather than to be served!

288

It's impossible for two minds to think alike always. Stop expecting your spouse, to think like you or agree with you always. Stay focused on agreements and solutions instead of the disagreements and differences!

<u>289</u>

Love is not about finding your beloved. It's about finding the beloved you already are!

290

You'll become your spouse's true friend, when you first become your own true friend!

291

When you hold back forgiveness, you hold yourself back, by staying stuck in the past!

292

If you want to enjoy a life filled with love, just choose to live a life full of Love!

293

You'll experience life beyond all boundaries, when you become the 'Love' that knows no boundaries!

294

You can end all fears in your marriage once and for all with Love - Fear ends when Loving begins!

295

Perfect Love makes the imperfections in your relationship perfect!

296

Marriage is your soul's solemn pledge and promise, to love your spouse and bring out the best in him or her, as long as you live!

297

A life lived without eyes to see, ears to hear, nose to smell and tongue to taste, is better than a life lived with a heart that could not Love!

298

Love is the essence of
life that keeps it fresh.
Keep your Marriage
Fresh by keeping your
Love fresh!

299

Love is not something physical you desire. It's the spirit of life, that desires to express through you!

300

Marriage is a game of love you play with your beloved, where there are no losers – You both Win!

301

It's your imagination and creativity that keeps the fun and excitement alive in your Marriage - not your logic or reason!

302

The most beautiful and precious gift you offer in in your Marriage is: YOU. Make sure you stay beautiful and precious!

303

The reward you get from the Universe in return for your Love is: MORE LOVE!

304

The only thing on this planet, that can make your Marriage more beautiful is: LOVE!

305

Your soul's deepest desire is, to be a blessing to your spouse and everyone you encounter on your path of life!

306

Remember, your worth in your Marriage is not determined by the amount of money you have. It's determined by the amount of Love you give!

307

When you appreciate similarities and accept differences, you transform your Marriage into a beautiful haven of love and understanding!

308

A loving Marriage can only be built and never be 'bought'. Build it with your devoted 'time' and 'attention'!

<u>309</u>

Peace is the finest essence of your inner most being. When your mind keeps its peace, it keeps its connection with its finest essence , to help you create your finest life!

<u>310</u>

The more you move out of your comfort zone and make yourself vulnerable, the more venerable you become in your relationship!

311

You'll get what you've always got, if you do what you've always done. If you want to get what you haven't got, you have to do what you haven't done!

312

Keep your Marriage constantly renewed by letting go the 'old' and letting in the 'new'!

313

You are together with your spouse today, because, it was meant to be and could not be any other way!

314

When you focus on what you are 'getting', you suck the juice out of your relationship. When you focus on what you are 'giving', you make your relationship 'juicy'!

315

Your Marriage is like a home. When something stops working, you don't buy a new home. You fix what's not working!

316

Keep this fundamental Marriage rule etched in your heart: Never 'say' or 'do' anything to your spouse, you'll never 'say' or 'do' to yourself!

317

Unconditional love transforms your Marriage into a divine temple of love and healing!

318

Success in your Marriage is not determined by the number of promises you make. It is determined by the number of promises you keep!

319

A great Marriage is your greatest assets on this planet. Protect and preserve it at all cost!

<u>320</u>

Complete dependence on your spouse for all your needs, is a recipe for unhappiness in your Marriage. Learn to manage both independence and interdependence wisely, to keep your relationship happy!

321

If you wait for your partner to change to be happy, you'll probably wait your whole life!

322

The more you enjoy your relationship with your spouse, the more you'll enjoy life. Go the fullest depth possible in your Marriage to enjoy life to the fullest!

323

The greatest gift you can bring into your Marriage is your willingness to focus on 'agreements' instead of 'disagreements'!

324

Y ou make your
Marriage better, when
you make your partner's
life better!

325

It's best to avoid making mistakes in your Marriage. If you do, be sure to never repeat them!

<u>326</u>

When you have nothing to hide, you'll have nothing to fear in your Marriage. Be open and honest with your spouse!

327

What matters most in your Marriage is, not how it looks from the outside. What matters most is, how it looks from the inside!

328

Pay attention to what you 'do' in your Marriage. Your actions always speak louder than your words!

329

Strong people lift people up and weak people put people down. Be the strong person in your Marriage!

<u>330</u>

In a loving Marriage, you don't try to walk 'ahead' or 'behind' your spouse. You walk 'with' him or her like a true friend!

331

The best way to add 'color' and 'variety' to your Marriage is to let your spouse be himself or herself!

332

A truly open Marriage

opens up everything

that's truly worth living

for in this life!

333

Take a mental vacation to be fully present emotionally with your spouse every day. This will help build an emotionally strong Marriage!

334

Always remember this
Marriage rule: Listen
before you speak, think
before you act, wait
before you criticize and
try before you give up!

335

Just like your past actions determined the present state of your Marriage, your present actions will determine its future state!

336

Your love for your spouse may not change the world but it may change the world for your spouse!

337

Instead of always trying to fix broken things in your Marriage, try to start things over, to create something better!

338

You become truly capable of loving your spouse, when you become truly capable of loving yourself!

339

It's not often the 'big' things that make a big difference in your Marriage but the 'small' things!

340

Smiles will add miles

to your relationship.
Learn to smile together
often!

341

The best way to deepen your relationship with your spouse is to deepen your understanding of him or her. The best way to understand him or her is through listening and careful observation!

342

Don't take yourself too seriously in your Marriage. Your marriage is not about you, it's about your spouse!

343

Just as fire purifies gold, difficult times help purify your Marriage. Allow the fire of difficult times, to make your relationship golden!

344

Remember, your relationship is better off without you, if you are not capable of making it better by being in it!

345

Your Marriage is like a Bank. The more deposits you make into it, the more you can withdraw in times of need!

346

A long road never feels long in good company. This is the best secret to a long-lasting Marriage!

347

There is no 'right' or 'wrong' in your Marriage. You are both right from each other's perspective. Your ability to see your partner's perspective, adds more depth and meaning to your relationship!

348

Your Marriage thrives where there is flow of 'positive' energy. Love, Acceptance and Forgiveness, keep the positive energy flowing in your relationship!

349

Stop expecting your spouse to be 100% perfect and start accepting him or her for who he or she is. No one is 100% perfect (including yourself)!

350

Remember, 'Words' and 'actions' are building blocks that build trust in your Marriage!

351

Care is the ingredient
that makes your
Marriage most flavorful!

352

The happiest people have no time to compare their Marriage with others. They are busy making their own Marriage happy!

353

A 'full-filled' Marriage requires two people giving their 'Full' 100%!

354

The greatest gift you can give your spouse in life, is a joyful relationship. The greatest gift you can give yourself, is also a joyful relationship!

355

Forgiveness is the best way to find peace. When you forgive, you find peace!

356

Whether you live in a 'loving' or 'unloving' Marriage has nothing to do with your spouse. It depends entirely on how you relate to your spouse and everything in your Marriage!

357

You cannot be a true 'Friend' in your Marriage, if you always listen with your 'head' and never with your 'heart'!

358

What matters in your Marriage is not what you do. What matters is, the 'love' and 'thoughtfulness' you put into what you do!

359

Be honest and truthful in your Marriage. There are no substitutes for honesty and truthfulness on this planet!

360

Your goal in your Marriage should be to make a difference in your partner's life and not your own!

361

Conversations are like food you serve in your Marriage. Keep your conversations healthy and tasty!

362

When you truly love your spouse, you'll make every effort to make him or her happy!

363

In a great Marriage, people focus on 'solutions' not 'problems'!

364

Never stop exploring or learning something new together with your spouse every day This brings new joys and new ways of connecting in your relationship!

365

Remember, your
Marriage is a
performance stage for
you and your spouse, to
express each other's
divine luminance!

Wishing you the best

marriage - filled with

utmost love, excitement,

joy, peace, fulfillment

and abundance!

With Love

Roy John

NOTES

NOTES

NOTES

NOTES

NOTES